POEMS.

POEMS

BY

JAMES T. FIELDS.

BOSTON:
WILLIAM D. TICKNOR & COMPANY.
MDCCCXLIX.

BOSTON:
THURSTON, TORRY & EMERSON,
31 Devonshire Street.

CONTENTS.

THE POST OF HONOR.

PRONOUNCED BEFORE THE BOSTON MERCANTILE LIBRARY ASSOCIATION, NOVEMBER 15, 1848.

THE POST OF HONOR.

WHEN yon old tower proclaims the impatient Nine,[1]
And Temple belles to homeward nooks incline, —
When airs are still, the organ pipes laid low,
And music's stream requested not to flow, —
When from his lips, whose mandates all obey,
The call rings out, admitting no delay, —
The bard, half conscious, rises to the floor,
And eyes the distance 'tween the desk and door;
He hoped some hand might kindly interpose
To veil the audience at the oration's close,

Some beam might start, some sudden false alarm
Might snatch a victim from the altar's harm;—
But, chained a captive at your chariot wheel,
To fail just now were hardly mercantile;
Promise to pay, you must endure the shock;—
There is no quarter after two o'clock.

No bright Aurora, with her cheerful smiles,
The evening minstrel on his way beguiles;—
Child of the Dawn, she bids her coursers fly
Through rosier blushes to the morning sky.
While thus the fingers of relentless Time
Hold hard and heavy at the reins of rhyme,
Thy leaden wings, O sleep-compelling power,
I hear descending from their shadowy bower;—
Spare, spare thy influence, cease thy drowsy calls
A few brief moments, till the curtain falls.

In boyhood's hour you bade my fluttering sail [2]
Spread its light canvas to the morning gale;

First, at your summons, with averted eye,
I felt the breeze that swept my pennant by;
I heard your echoes gathering on the shore,
As then I launched one childish pebble more; —
Still the old echoes linger in my brain,
And all those voices seem to live again,
As now I come, with more than boyhood's fears,
To mark the dial of our added years.
O, more than favored, could I meet to-day
The smiles that cheered my dim and faltering way;
O, more than blest, could I recall to-night
Those welcome forms that met my dazzled sight;
All the dear faces, all the buried past,
Too bright and brief, too beautiful to last.

Our vanished years! let Memory's muffled bell
Toll but one requiem, and but one farewell,
For him whose eyelids in a wintry grave [3]
Were closed in anguish by the icy wave.
Rest, early friend, bemoaned in life's young bloom,
Gone, like a shadow, to the voiceless tomb.

When last we climbed to yon high, leafy crest
To watch the sunlight fading in the west,
Ah, little thought I that this hand would trace
These words of grief above thy burial-place.
Thou hast our tears; but lo! the clouds depart,
Our brother sleeps with *sunshine* on his heart;
The storm has passed, the seas are silent now,
And Heaven's sweet smile has settled on his brow.

Our added years! What though to these we bow,
Farewell the Past! All hail the eventful *Now!*
What though grave fathers, still my friends, I meet,
Whose nursery floors are worn with little feet,—
What though, companion of my former years,
Thy face at market every morn appears,
While I, still ignorant as the greenest baize
What "goods domestic" go the greatest ways,
Grope blindly homeward to my noontide meal,
Unknowing what my damask may reveal;—
Heart leaps to heart, and warmer grasps the hand,
When Autumn's bugle re-unites our band!

That "virtue only makes our bliss below,
And all our knowledge is ourselves to know,"
We read at school, in unforgotten lines,
Where sterling sense in sparkling couplets shines;
My theme to-night *thy* glittering muse demands,
Who touched life's follies with unsparing hands,
Or thine, Urania, skilled to sweep the lyre [4]
With all Pope's freedom, and with Campbell's fire.

Star of the heart! the eagle's sunward plume!
Wild meteor, dancing in the midnight gloom,
Ambition's goal, that oft delusive dream,
The Post of Honor, is my chosen theme.
Its ampler range eludes my hurrying sight,
I can but hover, others may alight; —
Though far and wide the gleaming standard flies,
Wings clipt like mine can dare no upper skies.
But, though I come not with presuming hand
To scatter precepts, like a housewife's sand, —

Virtue's assassin, slander's bosom friend,
No verse of mine can flatter or commend.
The *humblest* muse should claim the *honest* line,
And swing no censer at corruption's shrine;
Unmoved by fear, should act no traitor's part,
Wear on her face the dial of her heart,
And dash aside, no matter who may hold
The poisoned chalice, though 't were made of gold.
Truth, ever sacred, counts that victory shame
Which clarions meanness to a world's acclaim;
Scorns the proud wretch who plays the fatal dart,
But, while he dallies, drives it to the heart;
Shuns the weak fool, whose eager gaze descries
His neighbor's faults with telescopic eyes;
Believes high rogues, though clad in jewels brave,
Should run the gantlet with the shabbiest knave, —
While *Honor's Post* should be for him secure
Who lets in sunshine at the poor man's door.

Unchanging Power! thy genius still presides
O'er vanquished fields, and ocean's purpled tides;

Sits like a spectre at the soldier's board,
Adds Spartan steps to many a broken sword;[5]
For thee and thine combining squadrons form
To sweep the world with Glory's awful storm;
The intrepid warrior shouts thy deathless name,
And plucks new valor from thy torch of fame;
For him the bell shall wake its loudest song,
For him the cannon's thunder echo long,
For him a nation weave the unfading crown,
And swell the triumph of his sweet renown.
So Nelson watched, long ere Trafalgar's days,[6]
Thy radiant orb, prophetic Glory, blaze, —
Saw Victory wait, to weep his bleeding scars,
And plant his breast with Honor's burning stars.
So the young hero, with expiring breath,
Bequeathes fresh courage in the hour of death,
Bids his brave comrades hear the inspiring blast,
And nail their colors, dauntless, to the mast;
Then dies, like Lawrence, trembling on his lip
That cry of *Honor*, "Don't give up the ship!"

Pageant of light, dissolving into air, —
Thou glittering folly, seeming only fair,
What myriad insects, crowding to the flame,
Die in the arena, cheated of thy name!
Go mark its influence o'er each scene of life,
Your neighbor feels it, and your neighbor's wife;
He o'er Columbia's District sees it shine,
While she, more modest, thinks a coach divine.
"Be rich, and ride," the buxom lady cries, —
"Be famous, John," his answering heart replies;
"The golden portals of the Chamber wait
To give thee entrance at the next debate;
Get votes, get station, and the goal is won,
Shine in the Senate, and eclipse the sun;
Quadrennial glory shall compensate toil,
The feast of office, and the flow of spoil."
Poor child of Fancy, party's candidate,
Born of a caucus, what shall be thy fate!
Nursed by a clique, perplexed I see thee stand,
Holding a letter in thy doubtful hand; —

It comes with questions that demand replies,
Important, weighty, relevant, and wise.
"Respected Sir," the sheet of queries runs,
In solid phalanx, like election buns, —
"Respected Sir, we humbly beg to know
Your mind on matters that we name below;
Be firm, consistent, that is, if you can;
The country rocks, and we must know our man.
And first, What think you of the Northern Lights,
And is it fatal when a mad dog bites?
Do you allow your corn to mix with peas,
And can you doubt the moon is one with cheese?
If all your young potatoes should decease,
What neighbor's patch would you incline to fleece?
When Lot's slow help-meet made that foolish halt,
Was she half rock, or only table salt?
And had the ark run thumping on the stumps,
Would you, if there, have aided at the pumps?
Do you approve of men who stick to pills,
Or aqueous pilgrims to Vermont's broad hills?

Do you mark Friday darkest of the seven?
Do you believe that white folks go to Heaven?
Do you imbibe brown sugar in your tea?
Do you spell Congress with a K or C?
Will you eat oysters in the month of June,
And soup and sherbet with a fork or spoon?
Towards what amusement does your fancy lean?
Do you believe in France or Lamartine?
Shall you at church eight times a month be found,
Or only absent when the box goes round?
Should Mr. Speaker ask you out to dine,
Will you accept, or how would you decline?
In case a comet should our earth impale,
Have you the proper tongs to seize his tail?
For early answers we would make request, —
Weigh well the topics, calmly act your best,
Show us your platform, how you mean to tread,
Plump on your feet, or flat upon your head;
If your opinions coincide with ours,
We delegate to you the proper powers.

N. B.—No bribes; the postage you must pay
From this to Boston, and the other way.
A Postscript, private.—If we all agree,
The undersigned expect the usual fee;
And if you publish in the Western Bull,
Pray do n't forget to print our names in full."

The ambitious guardian of the errant swine,
(Sometimes named hog-reeve by the sacred Nine,)
Think you no sighs his anxious breast denote,
Should chance divest him of his party's vote?—
Alas! he cries, with Wolsey in the play,
"Farewell, my greatness! Honor swept away!"
And feels, beneath that recreant party's frown,
A pang as great as when a king goes down.

The country curate, quoting Greek for gold,
Sees it resplendent o'er some distant fold;
His reverend locks, just turned of twenty-two,
Need other perfumes than a Cape Ann dew;—

Her ampler arms a City church extends,
He 'll be more useful there, he tells his friends;
He feels distressed, he goes with many a tear,
But yearns to practise in a wider sphere, —
Which, to interpret in a carnal sense,
Means a receipt of pounds instead of pence.
Go, worldly prophet! duty fling aside,
Your heart is Mammon's, and your worship Pride;
Ready to skulk when Progress might be taught,
Go hunt the Ibis of Egyptian thought, —
Leave Heaven for Tarshish, and you can 't but fail,
For every Jonah always finds his whale.

From pride of place his favor Honor turns,
And station only from his list he spurns.
At a late conference on a Hebrew word,
A Worcester blacksmith beat an English lord;
Think you he stooped, around *that* brow to bind
The waiting laurel due a titled mind?

No! "*Scots wha hae*" first thrilled with memories wild
The throbbing bosom of a ploughman's child,
And Ayr and Avon glide as gently still,
Though Burns and Shakspeare top the immortal hill.
Yon fountain Nymph, now sparkling through the trees,[7]
In humble Natick wooed the mountain breeze;
There, 'mid the torrent, nursed in thunders loud
From the dark bosom of the stormy cloud,
Or gentlier fed, when Summer's showery train
In drops of music poured the welcome rain,
Her lot was cast, content to glide along,
Lulled by the ripple of her own sweet song.
The Indian maids, her playmates, passed away,
And still she waited for a brighter day,
Till, all matured, she rose at Duty's call,
And stepped a Naiad in her charmèd hall, —
Sprang, crowned with grace, the monarch Elm beside,
And stood in radiant light his young enchanted bride.

Be great like Murray, but like Murray feel,
And thrice like him refuse the proffered seal;

Rome's cautious bard, of verse the lyric sage, [8]
Wrote *fuge magna* on his glowing page.
Greatness avoid! the throne has pangs to hide
That only lurk where kings and crowns abide.
Swing from the Common in your own balloon,
You may reach Marshfield in the afternoon;
But many a bog 'twixt here and Marshfield lies,
And gas may leak, and water fill your eyes.

All are not born the glory of their race,
But all may shun the pathway to disgrace;
In humblest vales the patriot *heart* may glow;
That nurtures *men* — *they* give the inspiring blow.
Point back to heroes battling for the right,
To modest martyrs dying out of sight,
When low-born cowards loitered in the dust,
And when 't was honored to be brave and just;
When gray-haired age with reverend footsteps trod,
And when sweet childhood learned to worship God;
When truth was sacred, and when men were rare
Who bartered Faith for nothing and Voltaire.

But does *our* pathway e'er conduct to fame?
The Merchant's honor is his *spotless name;*
Not circumscribed, just narrowed to the rank
That passes current only at the Bank,
But stamped with soul, howe'er the winds may blow,
Large as the sunlight, and unstained as snow.
Do good by stealth, be just, have faith in man;
The rest to Heaven, God always in the van, —
Though silent deeds may find no tongue to bless
Through the loud trumpet of the public press.

Honors, 'tis true, from no condition rise,
Stick to your calling, there the profit lies;
What man has sown, just what he reaps denotes,
Expect no pearl-ash from a crop of votes;
Oil and Cochituate never yet would mix;
You can 't pay rents and retail politics.

Consult your means, avoid the tempter's wiles,
Shun grinning hosts of unreceipted files,

Let Heaven-eyed Prudence battle with Desire,
And win the victory, though it be through fire.
Go swim at Newport to come home and sink
When the grim Notary drags you to the brink;
Play with old ocean, wanton as you will,
Time writes no wrinkles on a six months' bill.

Where lies true Honor? Turn the glass once more,
A few brief pictures, and the scene is o'er, —
All the procession may not pass to-night;
Enough if sketches show my purpose right.

The painter's skill life's lineaments may trace,
And stamp the impress of a speaking face;
The chisel's touch may make that marble warm
Which glows with all but breathing manhood's form,—
But deeper lines, beyond the sculptor's art,
Are those which write their impress on the heart.
On Talfourd's page what bright memorials glow [9]
Of all that 's noblest, gentlest, best below!

Thou generous brother, guard of griefs concealed,
Matured by sorrow, deep but unrevealed,
Let me but claim, for all thy vigils here,
The noiseless tribute to a heart sincere.
Though Dryburgh's walls still hold their sacred dust,
And Stratford's chancel shrines its hallowed trust,
To Elia's grave the pilgrim shall repair,
And hang with love perennial garlands there.
And thou, great Bard of never-dying name,
Thy filial care outshines the poet's fame;
For who, that wanders by the dust of Gray
While memory tolls the knell of parting day,
But lingers fondly at the hallowed tomb,
That shrouds a parent in its pensive gloom,
To bless the son who poured that gushing tear,
So warm and earnest, at a mother's bier!
Wreaths for that line which Woman's tribute gave,
"Last at the cross, and earliest at the grave."
Can I forget, a Pilgrim o'er the sea,
The countless shrines of Woman's charity?

In thy gay capital, bewildering France,
Where Pleasure's shuttle weaves the whirling dance,
Beneath the shelter of St. Mary's dome,
Where pallid suffering seeks and finds a home,
Methinks I see that sainted sister now [11]
Wipe Death's cold dew-drops from an infant's brow;
Can I forget that mild, seraphic grace
With heaven-eyed Patience meeting in her face?
Ah, sure, if angels leave celestial spheres,
We saw an angel dry a mortal's tears.

'T was thine, Jerome, when shuddering nature cried [12]
For aid and rescue from the burning tide,
'T was thine, with vigorous arm, and manly breath,
To leap through danger, and to snatch from death;—
Though prince and peer assumed their noblest mien,
Thou wert the Ocean Monarch of that scene.

Where e'er his camp-fires glistened on the sod,
Humane as brave, our latest Conqueror trod;
Honored not most when flying shaft and ball
Swept like red hail on Buena Vista's wall,

But for that aid a foot-worn soldier found
When limping wounded o'er the bloody ground, —
"My steed is thine," the pitying hero cried,
And lifted up a brother to his side.

Slow to applaud, our pulses rarely bound
When Genius walks his own enchanted ground,
While many a son, though hailed in distant lands,
Receives no chaplet at our tardy hands.
Not thus, on other soil, true greatness pines,
Not thus old age to poverty declines;
See Worth advanced, and power-compelling Mind
On some proud hill-top gloriously enshrined,
While sterling Merit leaves his lowly plain
To found a peerage, dated from his brain.
Yet, stern old shores, still on thy rocks they stand
Who guard the portals of our native land!
Our Country first, their glory and their pride,
Land of their hopes, land where their fathers died,
When in the right, they 'll keep thy Honor bright,
When in the wrong, they 'll die to set it right.

Let blooming boys, from stagnant cloisters freed,
Sneer at old virtues, and the Patriot's creed,
Forget the lessons taught at Valor's side,
And all their country's honest fame deride.
All are not such; some glowing blood remains
To warm the icy current of our veins,
Some from the watch-towers still descry afar
The faintest glimmer of an adverse star.
When faction storms, when meaner statesmen quail,
Full high advanced, our eagle meets the gale!
On some great point where Honor takes her stand,—
The Ehrenbreitstein of our native land,—
See, in the front, to strike for Freedom's cause,
The mailed Defender of her rights and laws!
On his great arm behold a nation lean,
And parcel empire with the Island Queen;
Great in the council, peerless in debate,—
Who follows Webster takes the field too late.[13]

Go track the globe, its changing climes explore,
From crippled Europe to the Arab's shore,

See Albion's lion guard her stormy seas,
See Gallia's lilies float on every breeze,
Roam through the world, but find no brighter names
Than those true Honor for Columbia claims.

Pause in that aisle, with half-suspended breath,
Where sceptered England shares her realm with Death,
And hear, beneath the Abbey's mouldering towers,
Her hoary minstrels chime the passing hours,
Then turn from halls, where blood-stained banners wave,
To peaceful Quincy and its new-made grave, —
From Pride and Power, enshrined in regal gloom,
To patriot Virtue, and to Vernon's tomb.

NOTES.

NOTE 1. PAGE 1.

The Annual Poem before the Mercantile Library Association is usually delivered on the same evening, immediately after an Address at the Tremont Temple.

NOTE 2. PAGE 2.

In boyhood's hour,

On a previous occasion, (in 1838,) the Anniversary Poem was recited by the author of the one now published.

NOTE 3. PAGE 3.

For him whose eyelids in a wintry grave,

Orlando Pitts, who was lost in the steamer Atlantic on the 27th of November, 1846. Among the many victims of that fearful storm, no one was more deeply lamented than the subject of these lines.

NOTE 4. PAGE 5.

Or thine, Urania,

It is scarcely necessary to explain this reference. Those who have read the admirable Poem pronounced in 1846 before the Society by Dr. O. W. Holmes, need not be reminded here of its excellence.

NOTE 5. PAGE 7.

Adds Spartan steps to many a broken sword;

"Mother!" said a Spartan boy, going to battle, "My sword is too short." "Add a step to it," was the heroic reply.

NOTE 6. PAGE 7.

So Nelson watched,

See Southey's glowing life of the great naval hero.

NOTE 7. PAGE 13.

Yon fountain Nymph, &c.

This passage refers to the beautiful jet so recently introduced to add its graceful beauty to Boston Common. The old Elm Tree, standing near the Pond, is too well known to require a further notice here.

NOTE 8. PAGE 14.

Rome's cautious bard,

"Fuge magna: licet sub paupere tecto,
Reges, et regum vitâ præcurre amicos."

HORACE.

NOTE 9. PAGE 16.

On Talfourd's page, &c.

The "Final Memorials of Charles Lamb," recently published by his eminent biographer, have added a new and solemn interest to the character of Elia. Such an exhibition of self-sacrifice under similar circumstances was never made before.

Note 10. Page 17.

And thou, great Bard of never dying name,

Gray lies buried in Stoke church, at the south-east corner of the chancel. He desired to be laid near the tomb of his mother, whom he had long and affectionately loved, and over whose remains the pilgrim to this interesting spot will read the following inscription, placed there by the author of the Elegy.

BESIDE HER FRIEND AND SISTER,
HERE SLEEP THE REMAINS OF
DOROTHY GRAY,
WIDOW, THE TENDER MOTHER
OF MANY CHILDREN, ONE OF WHOM ALONE
HAD THE MISFORTUNE TO SURVIVE HER.

Note 11. Page 18.

Methinks I see that sainted sister now,

Whoever has visited the Parisian hospitals, especially those devoted to the care of children, cannot fail to have learned a lesson not easily to be forgotten. The patient, gentle devotion of a young female, in the full flush of womanly beauty, to the wants of a dying orphan-infant, suggested this passage.

Note 12. Page 18.

'Twas thine, Jerome,

Some difference of opinion seems to exist with reference to this courageous sailor. That he worked manfully in the perilous scene to save those who were exposed to imminent danger, is a sufficient reason why his name should be honorably mentioned every where.

Note 13. Page 20.

Who follows Webster takes the field too late.

This closing line of the paragraph alluding to the great Statesman, was suggested by the well-known quotation : —

" Who follows Homer, takes the field too late ;
Though stout as Hector, sure of Hector's fate,
A wound, as from Achilles' spear, he feels,
Falls and adorns the Grecian's chariot wheels."

MISCELLANEOUS POEMS.

MISCELLANEOUS POEMS.

FAIR WIND.

O, WHO can tell, that never sailed
  Among the glassy seas,
How fresh and welcome breaks the morn
  That ushers in a breeze!
"Fair Wind! Fair Wind!" alow, aloft,
  All hands delight to cry,
As, leaping through the parted waves,
  The good ship makes reply.

While fore and aft, all staunch and tight,
  She spreads her canvas wide,
The captain walks his realm, the deck,
  With more than monarch's pride ; —
For well he knows the sea-bird's wings,
  So swift and sure to-day,
Will waft him many a league to-night
  In triumph on his way.

Then welcome to the rushing blast
  That stirs the waters now, —
Ye white-plumed heralds of the deep,
  Make music round her prow !
Good sea-room in the roaring gale,
  Let stormy trumpets blow ;
But chain ten thousand fathoms down
  The sluggish calm below !

ON A BOOK OF SEA-MOSSES,

SENT TO AN EMINENT ENGLISH POET.

To him who sang of Venice, and revealed
How Wealth and Glory clustered in her streets,
And poised her marble domes with wondrous skill,
We send these tributes, plundered from the sea.
These many-colored, variegated forms
Sail to our rougher shores, and rise and fall
To the deep music of the Atlantic wave.
Such spoils we capture where the rainbows drop,
Melting in ocean. Here are broideries strange,
Wrought by the sea-nymphs from their golden hair,
And wove by moonlight. Gently turn the leaf.

From narrow cells, scooped in the rocks, we take
These fairy textures, lightly moored at morn.
Down sunny slopes, outstretching to the deep,
We roam at noon, and gather shapes like these.
Note now the painted webs from verdurous isles,
Festooned and spangled in sea-caves, and say
What hues of land can rival tints like those,
Torn from the scarfs and gonfalons of kings
Who dwell beneath the waters.

Such our Gift,

Culled from a margin of the western world,
And offered unto Genius in the old.

BALLAD OF THE TEMPEST.

WE were crowded in the cabin,
  Not a soul would dare to sleep, —
It was midnight on the waters,
  And a storm was on the deep.

'T is a fearful thing in winter
  To be shattered in the blast,
And to hear the rattling trumpet
  Thunder, "Cut away the mast!"

So we shuddered there in silence, —
  For the stoutest held his breath,
While the hungry sea was roaring,
  And the breakers talked with Death.

As thus we sat in darkness,
  Each one busy in his prayers, —
"We are lost!" the captain shouted,
  As he staggered down the stairs.

But his little daughter whispered,
  As she took his icy hand,
"Is n't God upon the ocean,
  Just the same as on the land?"

Then we kissed the little maiden,
  And we spoke in better cheer,
And we anchored safe in harbor
  When the morn was shining clear.

SACO FALLS.

Rush on, bold stream ! thou sendest up
   Brave notes to all the woods around,
When morning beams are gathering fast,
   And hushed is every human sound ;
I stand beneath the sombre hill,
The stars are dim o'er fount and rill,
And still I hear thy waters play,
In welcome music, far away.
Dash on, bold stream ! I love the roar
Thou sendest up from rock and shore.

'T is night in heaven, — the rustling leaves
   Are whispering of the coming storm,
And thundering down the river's bed
   I see thy lengthened, darkling form ;

No voices from the vales are heard,
The winds are low, — each little bird
Hath sought its quiet, rocking nest,
Folded its wing, and gone to rest, —
And still I hear thy waters play,
In welcome music, far away.

The earth hath many a gallant show
  Of towering peak and glacier bright,
But ne'er beneath the glorious moon
  Hath nature framed a lovelier sight
Than thy fair tide, with diamonds fraught,
When every drop with light is caught,
And o'er the bridge the village girls
Reflect below their waving curls,
While merrily thy waters play,
In welcome music, far away!

ON A PAIR OF ANTLERS,

BROUGHT FROM GERMANY.

Gift, from the land of song and wine,—
  Can I forget the enchanted day,
When first along the glorious Rhine
  I heard the huntsman's bugle play,
And marked the early star that dwells
Among the cliffs of Drachenfels!

Again the isles of beauty rise;—
  Again the crumbling tower appears,
That stands, defying stormy skies,
  With memories of a thousand years,
And dark old forests wave again,
And shadows crowd the dusky plain.

They brought the gift that I might hear
  The music of the roaring pine, —
To fill again my charmèd ear
  With echoes of the Rodenstein, —
With echoes of the silver horn, —
Across the wailing waters borne.

Trophies of spoil! henceforth your place
  Is in this quiet home of mine; —
Farewell the busy, bloody chase,
  Mute emblems now of "auld lang syne,"
When Youth and Hope went hand in hand
To roam the dear old German land.

SLEIGHING SONG.

O SWIFT we go, o'er the fleecy snow,
  When moonbeams sparkle round ;
When hoofs keep time to music's chime,
  As merrily on we bound.

On a winter's night, when hearts are light,
  And health is on the wind,
We loose the rein and sweep the plain,
  And leave our cares behind.

With a laugh and song, we glide along
  Across the fleeting snow ;
With friends beside, how swift we ride
  On the beautiful track below !

O! the raging sea has joy for me,
  When gale and tempests roar;
But give me the speed of a foaming steed,
  And I'll ask for the waves no more.

SUMMER EVENING MELODY.

Go forth! the sky is blue above,
And cool the green sod lies below;
It is the hour that claims for love
The halcyon moments as they flow.

The glow-worm lends her twinkling lamp,
The cricket sings his soothing strain,
And fainter sounds the weary tramp
Of footsteps in the grassy lane.

Go forth, ye pallid sons of care!
Too long your thoughts to earth are given;
To-night sweet music haunts the air,
And fragrant odors breathe of heaven!

VILLAGER'S WINTER-EVENING SONG.

Not a leaf on the tree, — not a bud in the hollow,
  Where late swung the blue-bell, and blossomed the rose;
And hushed is the cry of the swift-darting swallow,
  That circled the lake in the twilight's dim close.

Gone, gone are the woodbine and sweet-scented brier,
  That bloomed o'er the hillock and gladdened the vale,
And the vine, that uplifted its green-pointed spire,
  Hangs drooping and sear on the frost-covered pale.

And hark to the gush of the deep-welling fountain,
  That prattled and shone in the light of the moon;
Soon, soon shall its rushing be still on the mountain,
  And locked up in silence its frolicsome tune.

Then heap up the hearth-stone with dry forest-branches,
  And gather about me, my children, in glee;
For cold on the upland the stormy wind launches,
  And dear is the home of my loved ones to me.

CHILDREN IN EXILE.

Two Indian Boys were carried to London not long ago for exhibition, and both died soon after their arrival. It is related that one of them, during his last moments, talked incessantly of the scenes and sports of his distant home, and that both wished earnestly to be taken back to their native woods.

Far in the dark old forest glades,
  Where kalmias bloom around,
They had their place of youthful sport,
  Their childhood's hunting-ground, —
And swinging lightly in the vines
  That o'er the wigwam hung,
The golden robins, building near,
  Above their dwelling sung.

Each morn their little dusky feet
  Sprang down the sparkling lea,
To plunge beneath the glowing stream
  Beside the chestnut tree;
And when the hiding squirrel's nest
  They sought, far up the hills,
They bathed their reeking foreheads cool
  Among the mountain rills.

They saw the early silver moon
  Peep through her wavy bower,
And in her beams they chased the bat
  Around his leafy tower;
And, when the stars all silently
  Went out o'er hill and plain,
They listened low to merry chimes
  Of Summer evening rain.

These haunts they missed, — the city air
  No healthful music brings, —
They longed to run through woodland dells,
  Where Nature ever sings;
And, drooping, mid the noise and glare,
  They pined for brook and glen,
And, dying, still looked fondly back,
  And asked for Home again.

A VALENTINE.

SHE that is fair, though never vain or proud,
More fond of home than fashion's changing crowd;
Whose taste refined even female friends admire,
Dressed not for show, but robed in neat attire;
She who has learned, with mild, forgiving breast,
To pardon frailties, hidden or confest;
True to herself, yet willing to submit,
More swayed by love, than ruled by worldly wit;
Though young, discreet,—though ready, ne'er unkind,
Blessed with no pedant's, but a *Woman's* mind; —
She wins our hearts, towards *her* our thoughts incline,
So at her door go leave my Valentine.

COMMON SENSE.

SHE came among the gathering crowd,
  A maiden fair, without pretence,
And when they asked her humble name,
  She whispered mildly, "Common Sense."

Her modest garb drew every eye,
  Her ample cloak, her shoes of leather, —
And when they sneered, she simply said,
  "I dress according to the weather."

They argued long, and reasoned loud,
  In dubious Hindoo phrase mysterious,
While she, poor child, could not divine
  Why girls so young should be so serious.

They knew the length of Plato's beard,
And how the scholars wrote in Saturn;
She studied authors not so deep,
And took the Bible for her pattern.

And so she said, " Excuse me, friends,
I find all have their proper places,
And *Common Sense* should stay at home
With cheerful hearts and smiling faces."

THE DEAD.

"Still the same, no charm forgot, —
Nothing lost that Time had given."

Forget not the Dead, who have loved, who have left us,
Who bend o'er us now, from their bright homes above;
But believe,— never doubt,— that the God who bereft us
Permits them to mingle with friends they still love.

Repeat their fond words, all their noble deeds cherish,
Speak pleasantly of them who left us in tears; —
Other joys may be lost, but their names should not perish
While time bears our feet through the valley of years.

Dear friends of our youth! can we cease to remember
  The last look of life, and the low-whispered prayer?
O, cold be our hearts as the ice of December
  When Love's tablets record no remembrances there.

Then forget not the Dead, who are evermore nigh us,
  Still floating sometimes to our dream-haunted bed;—
In the loneliest hour, in the crowd, they are by us;
  Forget not the Dead! oh, forget not the Dead!

TO A FRIEND.

Go, with a manly heart,
   Where courage leads the brave, —
High thoughts, not years, have stamped their part,
   Who shunned the coward's grave.

Clear, to the eye of youth,
   Their record stands enrolled,
Who held aloft the flag of Truth,
   Nor slept beneath its fold.

They heard the trumpet sound
   Where hosts to battle trod,
And marched along that burning ground ;
   Fear not ! they rest with God.

Like them advance in love,
  And upward bend thy sight;
Win Faith through Prayer; He rules above
  Who still protects the right.

DIRGE FOR A YOUNG GIRL.

UNDERNEATH the sod, low lying,
Dark and drear,
Sleepeth one who left, in dying,
Sorrow here.

Yes, they 're ever bending o'er her,
Eyes that weep;
Forms, that to the cold grave bore her,
Vigils keep.

When the summer moon is shining
Soft and fair,
Friends she loved in tears are twining
Chaplets there.

Rest in peace, thou gentle spirit,
    Throned above;
Souls like thine with God inherit
    Life and love!

EVENTIDE.

WRITTEN IN THE COUNTRY.

THIS cottage door, this gentle gale,
Hay-scented, whispering round,
Yon path-side rose, that down the vale
Breathes incense from the ground,
Methinks should from the dullest clod
Invite a thankful heart to God.

But, Lord, the violet, bending low,
Seems better moved to praise ;
From us, what scanty blessings flow,
How voiceless close our days : —
Father, forgive us, and the flowers
Shall lead in prayer the vesper hours.

A BRIDAL MELODY.

She stood, like an angel just wandered from heaven,
A pilgrim benighted away from the skies,
And little we deemed that to mortals were given
Such visions of beauty as came from her eyes.

She looked up and smiled on the many glad faces,
The friends of her childhood, who stood by her side;
But she shone o'er them all, like a queen of the Graces,
When blushing she whispered the vow of a bride.

We sang an old song, as with garlands we crowned her,
And each left a kiss on her delicate brow;
And we prayed that a blessing might ever surround her,
And the future of life be unclouded as now.

SONG.

All the splendid furniture of his late residence had been sold except his wife's Harp. That, he said, was too closely associated with the idea of herself; it belonged to the little story of their loves; for, some of the sweetest moments of their courtship were those when he had leaned over that instrument, and listened to the melting tones of her voice.

IRVING'S SKETCH BOOK.

Go, leave that harp! — twined round its strings
There 's many a magic spell:
Leave that untouched, — the strain it brings
This heart remembers well.

Let that remain! — all else beside
Go scatter to the wind!
The chords that won my home a bride
No other home shall find.

A BRIDAL MELODY.

SHE stood, like an angel just wandered from heaven,
  A pilgrim benighted away from the skies,
And little we deemed that to mortals were given
  Such visions of beauty as came from her eyes.

She looked up and smiled on the many glad faces,
  The friends of her childhood, who stood by her side;
But she shone o'er them all, like a queen of the Graces,
  When blushing she whispered the vow of a bride.

We sang an old song, as with garlands we crowned her,
  And each left a kiss on her delicate brow;
And we prayed that a blessing might ever surround her,
  And the future of life be unclouded as now.

It hath a power, though all unstrung
  It lies neglected now ;
And from her hands 't will ne'er be wrung,
  Till death these limbs shall bow !

It hath no price since that sweet hour
  She tuned it first, and played
Love's evening hymn within the bower
  Her youthful fingers made.

A spirit like the summer's night
  Hangs o'er that cherished lyre,
And whispers of the calm moonlight
  Are trembling from the wire ;

Still on my ear her young voice falls,
  Still floats that melody, —
On each loved haunt its music calls, —
  Go ! leave that harp and me.

The being she worshipped, as angels adore, —
  The bird she had nestled so close to her heart, —
That one! O, no other can ever restore
  The joy of her Eden, — from him she must part!

She must strive to forget him; and never again
  Send a dove to the world with the hope of return; —
She must close every portal, but sighing and pain
  In a bosom that sorrow can never unlearn!

BURIAL OF A GERMAN EMIGRANT'S CHILD AT SEA.

No flowers to lay upon his little breast,
  No passing-bell to call his spirit home,
But gliding gently to his place of rest,
  Parting, 'mid tears, at eve, the ocean foam.

No turf was round him, — but the lifting surge
  Entombed those lids that closed so calm and slow,
While solemn winds, like a cathedral dirge,
  Sighed o'er his form a requiem sad and low.

Ah, who shall tell the maddening grief of love
  That swept her heart-strings in that hour of woe? —
Weep, childless mother, but O, look above
  For aid that only Heaven can now bestow.

Gaze, blue-eyed mourner, on that silken hair, —
  Weep, but remember that thy God will stand
Beside thee here in all this wild despair,
  As on the green mounds of thy Fatherland.

SONG

OVER THE CRADLE OF TWO INFANT SISTERS, SLEEPING.

Sweet be their rest! no ghastly things
  To scare their dreams, assemble here;
But safe beneath good angels' wings
  May each repose from year to year.

Cheerful, like some long summer-day,
  May all their waking moments flow,
Happier, as run life's sands away,
  Unstained by sin, untouched by woe.

As now they sleep, serene and pure,
  Their little arms entwined in love,
So may they live, obey, endure,
  And shine with yon bright host above.

M. W. B.

THEY tell me thou art laid to rest,
  Companion of my happiest years!
That thou hast joined the loved and blest,
  Whose early graves are wet with tears, —
That I shall never hear again
  The voice that charmed my boyhood's ear,
Nor meet among the haunts of men
  Thy honest grasp of love sincere.

Friend of my youth! my buried friend!
  Thy step was gayest in the ring, —
My thoughts far back through childhood wend,
  And can I now thy requiem sing?

Alas! I feel 'tis all in vain, —
  Before such grief my spirits bow, —
Farewell! I cannot trace the pain
  That weighs upon my heart-strings now.

TO ONE BENEATH THE WAVES.

Come back from Memory's mourning urn,
  And bless my sight again;
For now in restless dreams I turn
  To clasp thy hand, — in vain!
I bid thy gentle spirit come
  And look once more on me;
But thou art slumbering where the foam
  Rolls madly o'er the sea.

Alas! how soon our better years
  To tempest winds are blown,
And all our hopes, and joys, and fears
  Alike are widely strown; —

She rests in yonder village-mound,
  Who should have been thy bride,
And thou art sleeping 'neath the sound
  Of ocean's flowing tide.

TO A PAINTER.

I 'VE sailed an ocean to behold the Rhine,
  That world of beauty bursting on the view, —
But now *your canvas wafts to me* the vine
  And rock-clad hills long since I wandered through.

Twin-castled River, far away no more, —
  What further need the Atlantic wave to plough ?
You 've brought old Coblentz to my very door,
  And Ehrenbreitstein is my neighbor now !

TO A MALIGNANT CRITIC.

Rail at him, brave spirit! surround him with foes!
  The wolf 's at his door, and there 's none to defend;
He 's as "poor as a crow;" give him lustier blows,
  And do n't be alarmed, for he has n't a friend.

Now twirl your red steel in the wound you have made,—
  His wife lies a-dying, his children are dead;
He 'll soon be alone, man, so do n't be afraid,
  But give him a thrust that will keep down his head.

He has n't a sixpence to buy his wife's shroud,
  He "writes for a living," so stab him again!
Raise a laugh, as he timidly shrinks from the crowd,
  And hunt him like blood-hound, most valiant of men!

Ha! finished at last;—there he hangs; cut him down;
  "A fine manly forehead!" I hear you exclaim;—
Now choose your next victim, to tickle the town,
  And your heart-pointed pen shall reap plenty of fame!

A WELCOME TO SAMUEL LOVER.

A WELCOME, Sam, throughout the land,
While roaming is your lot ; —
Reception *warm* we give to some,
To *you* we give it *hot !*

For ships are scarce, that anchor here,
Can boast a lad like you ; —
What is there, Sam, you never tried,
That *Handy* craft can do ?

Your voice, we know it well, Sam, —
We heard it long ago,
In the sweet-souled " angel's whisper,"
Where the " four-leaved shamrocks " grow.

And your merry laugh, we 've heard, Sam, —
  The hearty Irish roar, —
We held our sides with *Rory*, Sam,
  And now we cry for *More*.

'T is a greeting, Sam, unstinted,
  That we offer to the true, —
And a welcome, strong and hearty, Sam,
  Should meet a man like you.

LIFE AT NIAGARA.

AN EPISTLE FROM THE FALLS.

Dear N. : While the rainbows are spanning the Falls,
And a lusty Scotch infant next door raises squalls, —
While the frantic young mother shouts madly for milk,
In tones not so soft, quite, as satin or silk, —
Your friend, grown poetic, has snatched up his pen,
To dash off a line to " the best of young men."

You 've been at the Falls, and they can 't be described,
Though Coleridge himself from the tomb should be bribed;
Pile mountains of paper, and flood them with ink,
And Niagara is dry, though the reader should sink.
But there 's *life* here, my friend, — closely packed to be sure, —
For fashion condenses what man must endure :

Not a bed to be had, not a chair, or a block,
And the only spare table is old Table Rock.
How glorious a visit, were taverns and gongs
But banished a week to where Fashion belongs,
To tramp through the forest, with no charge of fares,
In a pair of brogans, such as Audubon wears;
To meet a lithe Indian, all stately and stark,
And "put up" a few days in his wigwam of bark; —
Gods! a walk through the woods, by the light of the stars,
Would outweigh all the lamps, and the Lewiston cars!

But here 's *life* at the Falls — from a year to fourscore —
(And I think by the sound there 's a *day* at next door;)
Here are members of Congress, away from their seats,
Though sure to be there when the dinner-gong beats;
Here are waiters, so eager your viands to snatch,
That they leap down the stairs like a multiplied Patch;
To the sound of sweet music they nimbly appear,
And whisk off your corn while they tickle your ear.
Here are pensive young preachers, dressed quite *comme il faut*,
In coats black as night, and cravats pure as snow;

Rich East India governors, heavy as gold,
Hanging round like weak sun-flowers, yellow and old;
Artistical talent, with sketch-book displayed,
Drawing very bad water in very poor shade;
Fat cockneys from Charing-Cross; belles from Madrid,
Whose long jewelled fingers outrival Jamschid;
Superb English maidens, with swan-swimming gait,
Who float round the Rapids like Junos in state;—
But the brightest-eyed daughters, the best string of pearls,
Represent in their beauty our own Yankee Girls.

Here cluster the fair, and the plain, and the prim,
Round the gallant and gay, whiskered up to the brim;
Here 's a biped in boots, a most exquisite ass,
Who looks at the Falls through a golden-rimmed glass;
And to-day such a waist, N., I saw on the Rock,
That to furnish the brains seemed a slight waste of stock.
Here 's a lively old lady, all feathers and fans,
Who trots about peddling her Susans and Anns;
And a drab-colored Quaker, I 've seen more than twice
Take a sly glass of something in water and ice.

But brief let me be, while the dull curfew tolls;
Niagara still lives! still it rushes, and rolls; —
There is no spot on earth where I'd sooner meet you,
And the friends we both love, N., the choice and the true,
Though a Downeastern editor published the lie
That this glorious old cataract's "all in my eye!"

THE ALARMÈD SKIPPER.

"It was an ancient Mariner."

Many a long, long year ago,
Nantucket skippers had a plan
Of finding out, though "lying low,"
How near New York their schooners ran.

They greased the lead before it fell,
And then, by sounding through the night, —
Knowing the soil that stuck, so well,
They always guessed their reckoning right.

A skipper grey, whose eyes were dim,
Could tell, by *tasting*, just the spot,
And so below he 'd "dowse the glim" —
After, of course, his "something hot."

Snug in his berth, at eight o'clock,
This ancient skipper might be found;
No matter how his craft would rock,
He slept — for skippers' naps are sound!

The watch on deck would now and then
Run down and wake him, with the lead; —
He 'd up, and taste, and tell the men
How many miles they went ahead.

One night, 't was Jotham Marden's watch,
A curious wag, — the pedlar's son, —
And so he mused, (the wanton wretch,)
"To-night I 'll have a grain of fun.

"We 're all a set of stupid fools
  To think the skipper knows by *tasting*
What ground he 's on, — Nantucket schools
  Don 't teach such stuff, with all their basting!"

And so he took the well-greased lead,
  And rubbed it o'er a box of earth
That stood on deck — (a parsnip bed) —
  And then he sought the skipper's berth.

"Where are we now, Sir? Please to taste."
  The skipper yawned, put out his tongue,
Then oped his eyes in wondrous haste,
  And then upon the floor he sprung!

The skipper stormed, and tore his hair,
  Thrust on his boots, and roared to Marden, —
"*Nantucket 's sunk, and here we are*
  Right over old Marm Hackett's garden!"

COMMERCE.

PRONOUNCED BEFORE THE BOSTON MERCANTILE LIBRARY ASSOCIATION, SEPTEMBER 13, 1838.

COMMERCE.

Harp of the sea! bold minstrel of the deep!
Sound from your halls where proud armadas sleep;
Ring from the waves a strain of other days,
When first rude Commerce poured her feeble rays;
Tell what rich burdens India's princes bore
Of balmy spices to the Arab's shore;
What mines of wealth on Traffic's dauntless wings
Sailed down from Egypt to the Syrian kings;
By what mischance, those wonders of their hour,
The fleets of Carthage, and the Tyrian power,
Were lost, and vanished like the meteor ray
That flashes nightly through the milky-way:

Sing of the Grecian States, that warlike band
Which held the ocean in its dread command;
Of Cæsar's glory, when his navies furled
Their sails before the granary of the world;
Of Afric's spoils by Vandals rent away,
And Eastern empires waning to decay.

Stand forth, old Venice — Genoa — Pisa — Rome!
With all your galleys on the crested foam;
Say, where are now your royal merchants seen?
Go ask the Red-Cross Knight at Palestine!

But lo! what crowds on Albion's shores arise,
Of noble fleets with costly merchandize;
What swift-winged ships rush in from every strand,
To swell the coffers of her teeming land,
While lofty flags proclaim on every breeze
The Island Queen, — the Mistress of the Seas!

Look to the West, — the Elysian borders view!
See where from Palos speeds yon wearied crew:

Haste, ere the vision to your eye grows dim,—
O'er rock and forest comes the Mayflower's hymn:
Fleet as the night-star fades in brightening day,
That exiled pilgrim-band has passed away;
But, where their anchors marked a dreary shore,
When first thanksgivings rose for perils o'er,
A nation's banner fills the murmuring air,
And freedom's ensign wantons gaily there.

O, glorious stripes! no stain your honor mars;
Wave! ever wave! our country's flag of stars!
Float till old Time shall shroud the sun in gloom,
And this proud empire seeks its laureled tomb.

Trace we the exile from his mother's arms,
Through traffic's din, its mazes and alarms;
And as remembrance paints his swift career,
From the rocked cradle to the noiseless bier;
A lesson learn,—that life's divinest gem
Is not wealth's boon or glory's diadem.

Look through the casement of yon village-school,
Where now the pedant with his oaken rule
Sits like Augustus on the imperial throne,
Between two poets yet to fame unknown:
While restless Horace pinions martyred flies,
Some younger Virgil fills the room with sighs;
Who, suffering now for one untimely laugh,
Ere long will write his master's epitaph;
Forgetting in his lines and comments bland
The painful ridges on his blistered hand.

And that small rogue, how slily he inweaves
The Pickwick papers with his Murray's leaves;
The race of nouns lies dim as sunken isles,
While Mr. Weller lights his face with smiles;
Or Mrs. Bardell weeps, — or lawyers plead, —
His task remains unconned, the wag will read.

Struggling with Colburn at the Rule of Three,
Yon pallid votary at the window see:

What though he linger, with a wistful eye,
Upon the dial as the sun mounts high ;
Impatient boy ! the man will soon complain,
Too swift the moments for his hours of gain ;
Too fleetly pass the sands of life away,
And death may claim him as a miser, gray.

Panting with joy to leave his native vale,
He leaps unarmed where scarce a veteran's mail
Would shield from sin in all its cunning forms,
Or keep secure where vice in legions swarms ;
Yet leaves he not his peaceful home unwarned,
Though many an earnest prayer perchance is scorned.

In fashion now, our hero strives to reign,
Sports the last hat, the latest Paris cane ;
Hangs out long clusters of superfluous hair,
And apes Lord Byron with his throat all bare ;
Makes one, perhaps, of that queer tribe of men,
Who play, in dress, part fool, part Saracen.

Behold him now, just launching into life,
Teeming with hope, with all her visions rife;
His youthful dreams stand forth in real forms,
The world before him, — he to brave its storms.
And think you now, as homeward oft he hies
From daily toil, no tears bedew his eyes?
Forgets he now the simple evening prayer,
Instilled in childhood by parental care?
Lingers not memory fondly round the place
His boyhood knew, lit by a sister's face?
Throbs not his heart with some keen darts of pain,
As he recalls his banished home in vain?
Ah! though long years some pangs away may steal,
There is a charm that he will always feel;
And, though Wealth's eye on Feeling coldly dwells,
And sneering points her to his hoarded cells,
That fairy Eden shall for ever smile,
And win him back with many a loving wile.

O, happiest he, whose riper years retain
The hopes of youth, unsullied by a stain!

His eve of life in calm content shall glide
Like the still streamlet to the ocean tide:
No gloomy cloud hangs o'er his tranquil day;
No meteor lures him from his home astray;
For him there glows with glittering beam on high
Love's changeless star that leads him to the sky;
Still to the past he sometimes turns to trace
The mild expression of a mother's face,
And dreams, perchance, as oft in earlier years,
The low, sweet music of her voice he hears.

The mails are in; lo, what cadaverous crowds
Are rushing now, like spectres from their shrouds;
In vain the dinner waits, the wife looks sad,
The children whine, the sweet-toned cook goes mad;
They stir not, move not from the busy walk,
But all is solemn as an Indian talk.
Say, would you tempt that earnest group to dine,
With smoking venison and the raciest wine?
Sooner will rabid men to fountains take,
Than those same worthies their intent forsake.

Go, ask them now to buy the last Gazette,
Or Daily Journal, while the council 's met ;
And, if in peace you wend your devious way,
You 'll swim unharmed the gulf of Florida !

Trade hath its bubbles ! Eastward where the sun
Throws off his night-cap when his nap is done,
Lo, how they rise ! what shouts on every hand
Proclaim the glories of our timber land !
O, who will credit such fantastic tales
While banks suspend, and India-rubber fails ;
While fancy-stocks hang trembling in the air,
And unwhipped rogues the guise of virtue wear ?

Hark, to the cry ! an embryo city dawns
On some dyspeptic in his morning yawns ;
Up spring tall forests in his magic dream,
And high-crowned turrets in the distance gleam ;
Short is his meal ; straightway a plan is drawn ;
Here lies a railroad, there a verdant lawn ;

Here steamboats land, and where, since time began,
A stagnant moat, ne'er visited by man,
Has stood unsung, unhonored in the shade,
Behold the changes in a morning made!

The stock sells well, the brewer quits his beer, —
Who picks up dollars when doubloons are near?
The shares go briskly off, the business thrives,
The shopman heeds not now his tens and fives;
For who would stop to measure calico,
While floods of gold through timber uplands flow;
Who sings a tune to three-and-six per yard,
While his next neighbour plays a nobler card?
Not he, indeed! ambition points the aim, —
He must keep horses, and grow fat on game.

Mark now the fall! Before the season 's late,
Our wealthy lord must visit his estate;
And, as his jaunt will raise some small alarms
Among the tenants of the adjoining farms,

He takes the statutes of the State of Maine,
His new brown coat, his golden-headed cane,
Kisses his children, bids his wife adieu,
And ere he knows it, half his journey 's through.
With map unrolled, he leaves the village inn,
Looking like Fusbos when he conquers Finn;
Meets on his way some tiller of the ground,
Perhaps his own — who knows? — he 's hale and sound.
The great man stops, the yeoman rolls his quid,
Nor doffs his beaver, as the landlord did.
"Are you employed, Sir, on the John Smith Farm?"
Our shopman asks, his anger waxing warm.
"They say John Smith owns yonder swamp down there,"
Replies the ploughman, straightening out his hair;
"But, as to farming, it is very clear,
He 'll find more black snakes than potatoes here."

O, short-lived bliss! the shopman looks around,
And finds his farm a tract of barren ground;
His forest trees to dwarfish shrubs decline,
His turrets vanish, nor can he divine

With what intent a railroad could be made
To such a spot, where neither lawn, nor glade,
Nor aught inviting to the expectant eye,
Relieves the dullness of a frowning sky.

The bubble 's burst! the dupe returns in haste,
Makes a small entry on his dusty waste,
Ere yet the rumbling of the mail has ceased,
" Profit and loss to cities lying east;"
And he who revelled on uncounted means,
Will sell his township for a mess of greens.

And is this all of life? I hear you ask;
Are there no flowers to deck our weary task?
Glows not the merchant's brow with more than these,
The hope of gain and wealth beyond the seas?
Cling not around his heart some happier ties,
Fraught with bright fancies, linked with warmer skies?
A slave to gold, must man in bondage toil,
And sweat for ever o'er the accursed soil?

There are, thank Heaven, beneath this fitful dome,
Some leaflets floating near affection's home;
Some cloudless skies that smile on scenes below,
Some changeless hues in life's wide spanning bow.
So let us live, that if misfortune's blast
Comes like a whirlwind to our hearths at last,
Sunbeams may break from one small spot of blue,
To guide us safe life's dreary desert through.

Time-honored city! be it ours to stand
In thy broad portals, armed with traffic's wand;
To keep undimmed and clear thy deathless name,
That beams unclouded on the rolls of fame;
And foster Honor, till the world shall say,
Trade hath no worthier home than yon bright bay.

But brief my lay; the fairy-land of song
Holds me a truant in its maze too long;
Yet chide me not, if, lingering on the shore,
I cast one pebble to the ripples more.

Our Yankee ships! in fleet career,
They linger not behind,
Where gallant sails from other lands
Court favoring tide and wind.
With banners on the breeze, they leap
As gaily o'er the foam,
As stately barks from prouder seas
That long have learned to roam.

The Indian wave with luring smiles
Swept round them bright to-day;
And havens to Atlantic isles
Are opening on their way;
Ere yet these evening shadows close,
Or this frail song is o'er,
Full many a straining mast will rise
To greet a foreign shore.

High up the lashing northern deep,
  Where glimmering watch-lights beam,
Away in beauty where the stars
  In tropic brightness gleam ;
Where'er the sea-bird wets her beak ;
  Or blows the stormy gale ;
On to the water's farthest verge
  Our ships majestic sail.

They dip their keels in every stream
  That swells beneath the sky ;
And where old ocean's billows roll,
  Their lofty penants fly :
They furl their sails in threatening clouds
  That float across the main, —
To link with love earth's distant bays
  In many a golden chain.

They deck our halls with sparkling gems
  That shone on Orient strands,
And garlands round the hills they bind,
  From far-off sunny lands ;
But we will ask no gaudy wreath
  From foreign clime or realm,
While safely glides our ship of state
  With Genius at the helm.

www.ingramcontent.com/pod-product-compliance
Lightning Source LLC
LaVergne TN
LVHW021429110826
845150LV00007B/2150